Charles Watkins

The Basilica : or, Palatial Hall of Justice and Sacred Temple :

its nature, origin, and a description and history of the

Basilican Church of Brixworth

Charles Watkins

The Basilica : or, Palatial Hall of Justice and Sacred Temple : its nature, origin, and a description and history of the Basilican Church of Brixworth

ISBN/EAN: 9783337260866

Printed in Europe, USA, Canada, Australia, Japan

Cover: Foto ©Lupo / pixelio.de

More available books at **www.hansebooks.com**

The Basilica;

OR,

PALATIAL HALL OF JUSTICE AND SACRED TEMPLE:

ITS NATURE, ORIGIN, AND PURPORT:

AND A

DESCRIPTION AND HISTORY

OF

THE BASILICAN CHURCH OF BRIXWORTH,

With Lithographic Illustrations.

BY THE

REV. CHAS. FRED. WATKINS,

VICAR OF BRIXWORTH;

AUTHOR OF "THE HUMAN HAND," "TWINS OF FAME," &c.

London,

RIVINGTONS, WATERLOO PLACE;

HIGH STREET, | TRINITY STREET,
Oxford. | Cambridge.

1867.

TO THE

RIGHT HON. EARL SPENCER, K.G.

DEAR LORD SPENCER,

The generous and handsome manner in which
you supported my endeavours for the Restoration of Brixworth
Church induces me to dedicate this Portion of my literary
labours for the explication of the Nature, Origin, and Purpose
of the Basilica in general, to your Lordship, as a tribute of
grateful respect from

Your Lordship's obliged and faithful Servant,

CHAS. FRED. WATKINS.

PREFACE.

I HAVE for many years been prepared with data for this Essay on the Basilica; but reserved the publication of any matter upon the subject till I could finish the excavations and discoveries pertaining to my own church, that I might bring out the descriptions of both together, as being cognate to each other. Not that I have been altogether silent on either subject. For in the year 1845, at the request of my old friend the Rev. T. Cooke, of St. Peter's, Brighton, I supplied a brief account of the church to my respected friend Canon Argles, for insertion in his well-known publication, the Cottager's Monthly Visitor, for which Mr. Cooke provided a south elevation.

B

Our Architectural Society desiring a lecture on the subject, and I still declining to treat it till I could do so more fully and certainly, the Rev. G. Ayliff Poole came over for the purpose, to whom I pointed out all that had been brought to light under my directions; and he being a profound Archæologist, and unprejudiced by the opinions of others, produced, with sound judgment, an excellent essay, more extensive than the epitome that I had sent for the Cottager's Monthly Visitor, but with some misconceptions, that I foresaw could only be settled by further investigations. This essay is inserted in our Architectural Journal. At the conclusion of his lecture, delivered to a large and intelligent annual meeting at the George Hotel, Northampton, I added, impromptu, a *vivâ voce* account of the Basilica, as I knew that the purport of the different parts of the church then described would not be clearly seen and fully appreciated without it.

Two or three years ago I carefully prepared an essay on the subject, after the investigation and study of many years, to be published with one on the church, as soon as I had an opportunity of examining, in all its parts, the construction and elaboration of the walls throughout the building. But having forwarded it for perusal to a gentleman versed in ecclesiastical and general art, and he having mislaid it beyond recovery in time for publication, I was obliged to recompose it as far as my memory served: and this at 72 years of age, and after a long and severe illness, amidst heavy professional and other labours, can hardly be so full and satisfactory as the original MS. In both Essays I have studied as much brevity as consists with perspicuity, approving the ancient maxim at all times, μέγα βιβλίον μέγα κακὸν, a great book is a great bore; and especially at the present day, when the very titles of the works published are enough to produce confusion and amazement.

Believing that the early Basilican type exhibits the best and truest principles of legal and ecclesiastical buildings, and the Church of Brixworth being the only one in this kingdom preserved from such great antiquity, with the whole ground-plan ascertained, and the main parts of the building still entire, will, I trust, be considered a sufficient warrant for adding these Essays to the multitudinous issues of the press.

BRIXWORTH,
15th April, 1867.

THE BASILICA,

&c.

THE Basilica, in its earliest and simplest form, was a rectangular building, apportioned into three squares, two undivided at one end, and one distinguished from them at the other end. Thus in a building ninety feet long, the larger division of two undivided squares would be sixty feet in length, by thirty in breadth; the smaller division would be thirty feet square. This measurement is of the central building only, exclusive of the peristyle, and requires to be constantly kept in mind; for every extension of outer works at equal distances from the main building alters the proportions and lessens the relations of length to breadth.

Before the commencement of the larger division, there was an atrium or square porch. At the other end of the building there was sometimes a semicircular apse or concha, so called from its resembling in shape a shell.

The origin and purport of such building would be to hold courts of justice in civil matters, and for the performance of sacred rites in the exercise of religious functions. In either case the necessity for a building of this kind is sufficiently manifest. For, in the administration of justice, the apse would be necessary to contain the bema or tribunal, somewhat raised above the rest of the building, on which the judge might sit, with his assessors near and below him.

The square portion nearest to the apse would be required for the advocates and their clients, and the larger portion beyond for the public auditory.

This tripartite division is still necessary and prevalent in our present courts of justice, though the separations are not so distinctly marked.

To this simple form of the hall of justice there were added lateral chambers opposite to the court of the advocates, into which they might retire for conference and arbitration; and these chambers had their respondents on the outside of the other end of the building for the use of the inferior officers attendant upon the court, and corridors of communication were erected between these terminal chambers.

If any one will search diligently into the remotest history of nations, he will find 'that the royal and sacerdotal offices were generally united in the same person : that he who one day would sit on the tribunal to administer justice, would at another time use it as a sacrarium for the performance of religious rites.

Amongst the numerous instances which might be adduced of the royal and sacerdotal functions being united in settled governments, is that of Crœsus, king of Lydia, who, by sacerdotal authority, expiated Adrastus. Also the Spartan kings, to whom the priesthood of the Lacedæmonian and celestial Jupiter pertained, and the back and skin of the victim as perquisites of the priesthood. Rameses, the sixth king of Egypt, is represented on the monuments of that country in the character of a priest offering incense. The custom still prevails in the Grand Lama of Thibet. The case of Melchizedek must present itself to all readers of the Bible; and He of whom Melchizedek was a proper type, our Great High Priest and Heavenly King. The readers of Virgil will recollect "Rex

Anius atque sacerdos." Samuel united in his person the threefold office of prophet, priest, and king; and David and Solomon assumed the priestly office in blessing the people.

In the exercise of religious worship, the first portion, next to the apse, was used by tho'se who assisted in the performance, whilst the larger area beyond would be occupied by the worshippers at large. And thus it was that when the Roman Empire was converted to Christianity, these Basilicas or Halls of Justice were found so convenient for Christian worship,—the bema serving for the Bishop's throne; the advocates' chambers serving for vestries; and the narrow corridors, being widened and enlarged, were converted into aisles, and afforded greater accommodation for the increasing congregations.

The Tabernacle in the wilderness affords us the earliest instance of the Basilica in its simplest form, being divided into three squares, a twofold and single. The whole length of the Tabernacle, from east to west, was thirty cubits: the sanctum ten cubits, or one-third of the whole, and the width ten cubits: the remainder twenty cubits or two squares. We have this on the testimony of Josephus. The three temples at Jerusalem successively exhibited, in the main body, the same divisions and proportions as the Tabernacle. In Leviticus vi. 1, we have given us these proportions of Solomon's temple.

The Basilican church of Brixworth has the same proportions. Mr. Edward Charles Hakewell, in his elaborate work on Ecclesiastical and Civil Architecture, refuses the testimony of Josephus as to the divisions of the Tabernacle: but what better authority could be wished for? and the agreement of its proportions with those of the national temples is strongly in its favour.

As their King was not upon earth, but in heaven, there was no occasion for apse or bema; and the single square was therefore made the sacrarium, or most holy place, where the high priest received the oracles of the Heavenly Monarch; and, in his vicarious capacity, transacted a sacrificial advocacy on behalf of the people. The holy place, answering to the chancel proper and court of advocates, was occupied by the priests and Levites, and the court without by the people.

It is indeed remarkable that some of the earliest of the heathen temples maintained this tripartite division of three squares:—that at Pæstum; the temple of Theseus; the temple of Jupiter; the temple of Esculapius, of Jupiter Stator at Rome, and of Neptune therein. In the temple of Pæstum, the sanctum was twenty cubits, the nave forty cubits, the width twenty cubits. See the ground-plan of Brixworth Church.

The aptitude which this Basilican form presented for the performance of both the civil and religious functions will account for this traditionary repetition from age to age, and will occasion its continuance to the end of time.

The human origin of this construction may be reasonably referred to the patriarchal government. For the father of the family was necessarily the ruler and priest of the household : his authority would afterwards merge into the head of the tribe; and he again would be superseded by that of the monarch when the extended tribes should be united under one sovereign. The manner in which the civil authority was thus transferred is circumstantially related by Herodotus in the case of Deïoces.

And Layard discovered in Nineveh the ground-work of a Basilica of the same construction as the church at Brixworth. Additions were made in some of the earliest temples of peristyles, porches, &c.; and in the Byzantine Basilicas of a late date, accessions were made to the more simple form by galleries, triforia, &c., to the lessening of that impressive grandeur which characterizes the earlier type; and it was remarked by those who had seen the first St. Peter's, that it far excelled the more elaborate and ornate production of Bramante in this respect.

In the provincial towns the apse and intermediate part were made to answer the purposes of municipal government, and the larger portion those of a covered market-house.

Beneath the semicircular apse there was frequently a crypt. This in the Roman Basilica was used for a prison. The following description of such a subterranean prison is taken from Sallust:

"There is a place in the prison, after a small descent to the left, called Tullus's dungeon, sunk about twelve feet underground, with an arch of stone, a dark noisome solitude frightful to behold." In Christian churches they were used for religious services, and as burial-places for sainted persons.

SYMBOLISM.

And as there was a general adaptation in the form of the structure to the civil and religious wants of mankind, so was there a symbolism involved in that structure, which, with respect to the Tabernacle at least, cannot be denied. For Moses was commanded to build the Tabernacle in the following words:—" Look that thou make them after their pattern which was shewed thee in the mount [1]."

And St. Paul, in his Epistle to the Hebrews (viii. 5), says of the priests under the law that they serve unto the example and shadow of heavenly things, as Moses was admonished of God when he was about to make the Tabernacle: for " See, saith he, that thou make all things according to the pattern shewed to thee in the mount." Thus, therefore, there is not only a symbolism declared, but a symbolical representation of heavenly things expressly stated. And as in the general, so with the particulars is that symbolism recorded; for the innermost of the tripartite divisions, or Holy of Holies, or Most Holy Place, is compared to Heaven itself, the entering into which by the high priest once a year, with the atoning blood of the burnt-offering, being declared symbolical of the Saviour entering into the highest heavens, with the all-sufficient virtue of His own

[1] Exod. xxv. 40.

most precious blood. The Tabernacle itself represented His sacred body, the veil His flesh.

Furthermore, St. Paul himself divides the heavens into three successions, having himself had a vision of the third heaven, wherein he saw what might not be uttered by the tongue of man. The partition wall also was made to represent the line of demarcation between the two covenants, and between their respective worshippers, which was broken down by Christ, when he proclaimed salvation to the Gentiles, and admitted them within the pale of the Christian Church. Josephus, as Jewish writers in general, and some Christian authors likewise, carries symbolism to a great extent; but I go not beyond unquestionable authority.

The form and proportions of the early Basilicas having been described, I proceed to explain the different materials used in the erection of the building, and indeed of all important edifices. These would greatly—I may say principally—depend upon the geological formation of the place. In all countries where there was an absence of rocky strata, the builders would follow the examples of those of Babel, using "bricks for stone, and slime for mortar;" and thus the

Basilica at Nineveh was built: thus the Roman Basilicas. And hence the necessity of the semicircular arch in those buildings and places.

But when a rocky stratum was near, large buildings especially would be erected of stone, and the openings be angular or rectangular; because the stones singly would serve for lintels as well as for side-posts. Thus in Egypt and Greece, the neighbouring mountains supplying them with these materials at hand, the doors and windows generally obtained a rectangular form, or inclined in Egypt to the trapezium; though the semicircular arch, and the equilateral were sometimes adopted by that people: hence the immense obelisks, colonnades, and statues of that country, from the facilities which the mountains afforded. Whereas on the banks or the Tiber and the Thames, the buildings are generally of brick from the neighbouring clay; although where expense is not a great object, the stones of far-distant quarries are transported by sea and by land for the purposes of architectural beauty, sculptured illustrations, and permanent duration.

Some of the earliest buildings after the Flood were composed of vast glacial, diluvial, or alluvial blocks, which, lying on the ground ready at hand, were first made use of, and especially by immigrants coming from a distance, not without the knowledge, but destitute of the appliances in the art of building :—thus the Titanian walls, the Druidical and other like erections of large stones, with only mortice and tenon to uphold the transverse layers, but neither hewn nor close-jointed. And where there was a choice of clay for bricks, and loose rubble for walls, the latter was often selected, or both together used, the excellency of the mortar rendering the concrete as hard as iron. Sir Grenville Temple ascertained the cisterns of Carthage to have been composed of this material ; and sometimes walls constructed of small and thin stones were erected with those stones in an oblique and converse manner, called "herring-bone work," as may be seen in the square and round towers of Brixworth Church.

The Egyptian semi-trapezium resolved itself into the pointed arch, and the semicircular arch contracted itself into the post-Norman transition arch. The Early English, as it is called, expanded into the Decorated, the Decorated into the Tudor : and these were all varied in construction and ornamentation.

The three pure and simple styles are the semicircular, the rectangular, and the equilateral. All the others are divergencies and modifications. In reviewing the history of those buildings which, whether with " cloud-capped towers, and lofty pinnacles," and pointed spires, or in greater simplicity of structure, have passed away, one can hardly avoid a thought respecting the fate of those, and the communities to which they belong, that now exist. Macaulay's image of the New Zealander, sitting upon London Bridge and soliloquizing on the ruins of the Capital, which has obtained so much currency and admiration, may perhaps occur to the reader's mind. It is not by any means an original idea of our florid historian. He gained it from a more imaginative and eloquent writer, Volney, in his dazzling, but deceptive work, " The Ruins of Empires," who places himself amidst the wreck of Palmyra, and soliloquizes on the anticipated ruins of London and Paris. *Suum cuique.*

Let us hope that the Spirit of Christianity will preserve the Capital of this Christian country from the occasion of any such soliloquies.

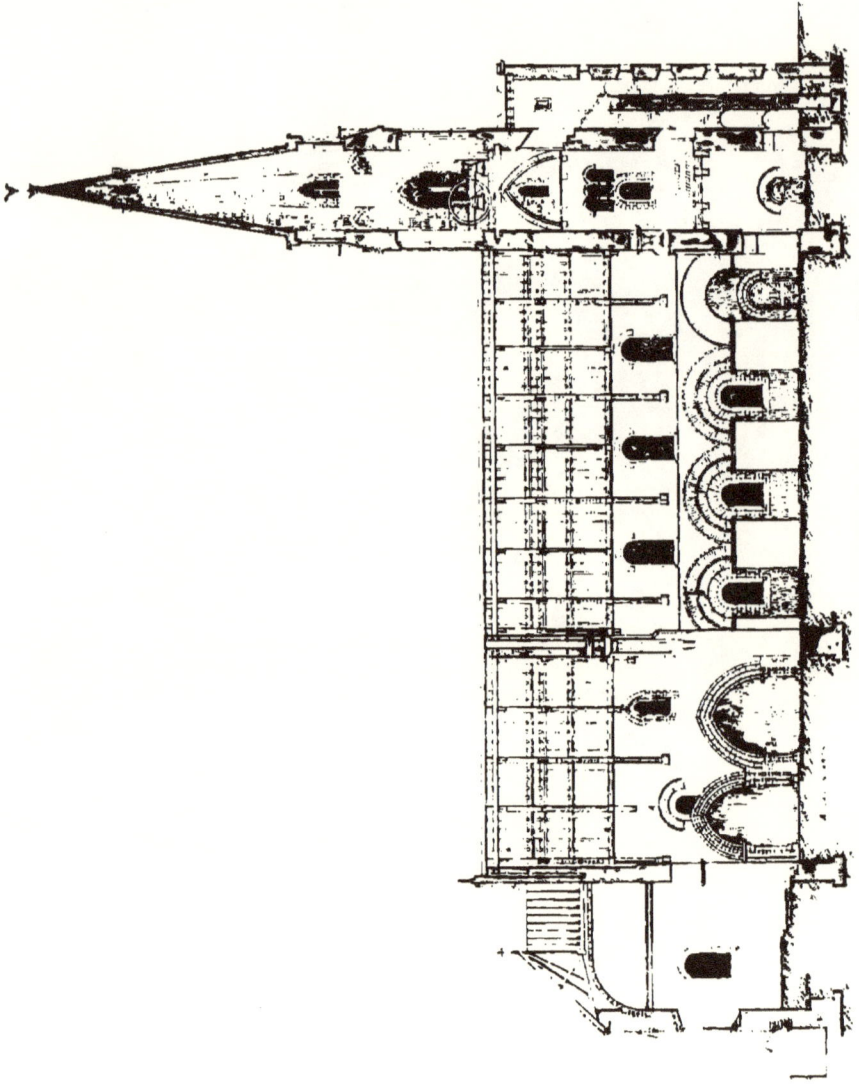

THE BASILICAN CHURCH OF BRIXWORTH.

With Lithographic Illustrations.

C.

TO

SIR CHARLES EDMUND ISHAM, BART.

THE Dedication of this Work on Brixworth Church is clearly due to you, as the Restoration of that ancient and interesting building is more indebted to the kind and generous efforts of Lady Isham and yourself than to any one besides. And I avail myself of this call of Justice, for the expression of other pleasurable, as well as grateful sentiments, to one whom I have known from early youth, in whom I soon discerned the early pursuit of knowledge for a future well-stored mind, and a refined taste for the elegant and useful Arts of Life, with a disposition to those better qualities which have endeared Lamport Hall and its inmates not to its own neighbourhood only, but far and wide through a great part of the County at large. That health and happiness may ever prevail therein is the sincere prayer and wish of

Yours truly,

CHAS. FRED. WATKINS.

BRIXWORTH VICARAGE,
March 29, 1867.

INTRODUCTION.

I CANNOT do better than reprint my address to the British Archæological Association at their excursion to Brixworth Church :—

[Extracted from the *Northampton Herald* of Saturday, August 16, 1862.]

On the Friday morning a special train brought between thirty and forty of the members, including the president, Dr. Lee, the secretaries, J. R. Planché, Esq., E. Roberts, Esq., Messrs. Wright, &c., and some ladies, to the Brixworth station, from which all who desired were brought up in carriages, sent by the vicar and the principal parishioners for their service. They were met at the church by the vicar and several of the county families and their friends, including Sir Charles and Lady Isham, the Hon. and Rev. Arthur and Mrs. Douglas, the Hon. Henry and Lady Mary Douglas, Henry O. Nethercote, Esq., and Mrs. Nethercote, the Rev. J. L. Roberts, vicar of Spratton ; — Lacon, Esq., and Mrs. Lacon ; and others belonging to the parish and neighbourhood. On the party being seated in the church,

The Rev. C. F. Watkins gave a very interesting *vivâ voce*

account of the church. He expressed the pleasure he felt in
receiving them within those venerable walls, and thought the
best course he could pursue, sanctioned as it had been by Mr.
Pettigrew, on whom they greatly relied, was to give them a
brief and simple statement of the manner in which he had
pursued his investigations into the remains of the ancient
building, till he had entirely ascertained and developed the
whole of the original plan.

It is now thirty years (proceeded the reverend gentleman)
since I took possession of this living, and I was naturally
struck with the singular appearance of this building—its
arches formed of Roman bricks, and every subsequent style
of architecture interposed up to the time of Henry VI. The
only notice that had previously been taken of the church was
by Mr. Britton, that energetic and useful pioneer in archæological matters, and Rickman, the writer on Gothic architecture,
both of whom had their attention called to the building by
Mr. Baker, the late historian of the county, and his sister.
Through the exertions of the latter, some of the brick arches
were scraped and laid bare, and part of the foundation of the
outer wall to the north aisle ascertained, but nothing was done
to develope the original plan of the building, nor was any plan
suggested.   Mr. Britton concluded it to have been an Anglo-
Roman building—Mr. Rickman, a Norman ; it appears, however, as deduced by Mr. Roberts, from the edition of his book
in 1835, eleven years after he had visited Brixworth, that he
then classed it amongst the Saxon buildings of the country,
though not earlier than those of Barton-on-Umber and Earl's
Barton.

After long careful examination, and mature consideration, I
concluded it to have been originally built for a Roman Basilica
or hall of justice, or rebuilt by the early Saxons after the
Roman type.   I met with little encouragement and much
opposition in proposing this view.   There was at that time
a prevailing prejudice against the supposition of the existence

of early remains of Saxon architecture of any account, or of any thing prior to the Norman period. A hundred years ago prejudice ran the contrary way. If an arch was discovered with any tracery, especially with any chevron work, it was immediately attributed to the Saxons. When that error was exploded, the prejudice ran in a contrary direction, as is usual with mankind, and the Saxons were reported as incompetent for any considerable work.

The late Marquis of Northampton—a man of remarkable sagacity and acumen—and the late rector of Orton Longville, who had examined all the architectural remains in Italy and the rest of the Continent, alone encouraged me in this view. The first thing I did was to take occasion of the burial of a parishioner in the chancel to make excavations there. I observed in the north-western corner of the exterior two sides remaining of a former polygonal structure, and noticed that the interior of that part curved a little. This led me to infer that it was part of an original apse, polygonal without and semi-circular within, and probably with an underground crypt, as in the oldest forms. I therefore made the masons prolong their excavations, till they reached, as I suspected, a subterranean wall, ten feet deep, which I made them lay open in its whole extent, till it came to view a perfect semicircle, and I left it open for public inspection from two to three months. But being obliged to close it up, for the performance of the sacred rites, I determined to work in a different quarter. Having observed an opening at the east end of the subterranean wall, I concluded there must have been also a subterranean chamber or corridor on the outside of the wall, for this source of communication; and if a corridor, or ambulatory, as it is sometimes called, a descent to it from the east end of the church. Accordingly, I had the wall at the north-east corner pierced and opened; and, after some labour and risk, succeeded in laying bare a circular-headed doorway, from which I doubted not there had been a descent to the cavity below. A serious obstacle presented itself to any investigation without, in the form of a solid embankment as high as the present window. But, after removing about 200 loads of earth, I had the satisfaction of revealing the outer wall of the crypt, the doorway and original steps of descent, an outer low subterranean wall encircling the corridor in parallel lines with the interior of the original apse, with a recess in one of the sides, receiving a vaulted roof, which sprung from the string course of the wall of the crypt. My next object was to lay open what I concluded would prove to be the north aisle with its apsides, which the respective arches seemed to indicate as having existed. Another embankment of earth, up nearly to the windows, again proved an obstruction, but I at length succeeded in laying open the whole aisle, coterminous with the nave, subdivided by foot buttresses, with a terminal square apse at the east end, and a rectangular one at the west, the latter formed by the recess from the nave to the square porch. On the south side, where greater obstructions presented themselves in more recent buildings, I made sufficient investigations to assure myself of corresponding parts to those on the north. Thus, abstracting the circular tower at the west, which, by its straight joint and other features, is proved to have been a later appendage to the building, I at length ascertained and developed, what I had always inferred and suggested to others, a complete Basilican form in the original building, viz., a square porch, with a main west entrance, opening into apsides north and south, and into a nave with four arches of a side, these arches opening into corridors, and with clerestory windows above between each two of the four arches, a compartment at the east of the nave leading into a semicircular apse, and opening into square apsides, or terminals to the aisles, at its commencement from the nave. (See ground-plan.)

And now with respect to this compartment. It is evident that the walls on either side were originally without the present openings. The first that was made was the smaller arch on the south side, excavated for the purpose of communicating with the present south aisle, which was built in the early part of the 14th century, as a chapel for Sir John de Verdun, Lord of the Manor, whose effigy is now enclosed in an arched recess of the south wall of that aisle. Fifty years later the larger arch was opened, and the clerestory window above. In the north wall of this compartment a Decorated and a Tudor window were afterwards inserted ; the latter is now superseded by a Decorated window, substituted at the time of rebuilding the wall in that part.

If you look up to the commencement of the large arch which leads from the nave, continued Mr. Watkins, you will perceive the spring of an early brick arch, which was supposed— Rickman suggested this—to have spanned the whole width of the church ; but it is evidently too small for such a compass, neither is there sufficient pier to support such an arch. I suspected that it was only a small clerestory arch, corresponding to the opposite one at the east end, for the purpose of throwing light into the choir from the clerestory of the nave, as those at the east end did from without the building, and that there must have been a central or triumphal arch corresponding to that which leads into the chancel, with side walls and round-headed doors, and clerestory windows over them, in counterpart to the east end. On burying a corpse near to the crossing, I had the excavation continued, till I arrived at the bases of the central piers, thus verifying all that I had inferred respecting this building.

When Mr. Poole, several years ago, read a paper on Brixworth Church, before the members of our Architectural Society, at the George Hotel, Northampton, I added *vivâ voce* observations of a supplementary character, and some of them to this purport, that I was convinced that we should some day find the origin not only of the circular brick arch called the Roman, but of the Basilica itself, in the plains of Shinar. Some time afterwards on going to the British Museum to

inspect the slabs from Nineveh, I discovered the type of one
of our Saxon arches on one of the blocks, and beside it a
type of the Norman arch, with its chevron work. And I had
the satisfaction of subsequently hearing Mr. Layard describe,
at a meeting in the Mechanics' Institute, the foundation of a
Basilica in the ruins of Nineveh, corresponding in its several
details to that of Brixworth.

A STATEMENT OF THE RESTORATIONS IN BRIXWORTH CHURCH,
SUBMITTED TO THE COMMITTEE OF THE ARCHITECTURAL
SOCIETY, AT THEIR ANNUAL MEETING ON THE 11TH OF
DECEMBER, 1865, BY THE REV. C. F. WATKINS, VICAR OF
BRIXWORTH, AND A MEMBER OF THE COMMITTEE.

[Extracted from the *Northampton Herald* of Saturday,
December 16, 1865.]

MY DEAR COLLEAGUES,—In presenting you with a statement
of my proceedings and discoveries in the course of restoring
this venerable church, as preliminary to its being brought before the public, I feel that I am only paying due respect to
those who have been appointed the Executive Council of the
Architectural Society of this county. You were duly informed
by plans and prospectuses, that the work was to be done in
sections, as funds might be found, and the work to cease within
the limits of those funds. The first section was that of the
west end, forming two of the three squares of the nave, sixty
feet by thirty feet, and fifty feet high. In this section all the
Saxon arcade and clerestory windows are reopened, and re-
paired in the most substantial manner, every brick and stone

of the original work carefully preserved *in loco*, and the requisite repairs done with Boughton stone, which distinguishes the new work from the old, and yet will not unfavourably harmonize with the latter. In scraping the stucco and mortar off the walls, we found a large square block of free-stone built into the west pier of the western arch of the south side of the church, by the early Saxons, having a Roman eagle, of the Assyrian type, fairly sculptured on the exposed side, but very slightly injured, and in good relief. On the upper part of the stone are three mortices, showing that some ensign or other was fixed in above the eagles. On excavating the floor of the square tower, I discovered the bases of two circular columns on each side of the original west entrance, with a wall running from one of them towards the nave; forming the propylœum to an early Roman Temple or Christian Church of the four first centuries : charred wood and burnt stone showed this part to have been burnt with fire. These bases had been hacked on the outer side of each, to receive respectively the corpse of a full-grown person, who from being cramped up would appear to have suffered a violent death ; one of them was encased in mortar, and till exposed to the atmosphere, the teeth and bones had an appearance of great comparative freshness. Mr. Roberts, in his pamphlet on Brixworth Church, declares that the present square tower was a later appendage to the western wall of the nave, because, as he argued, the walls were straight-jointed; but this mistake of his arises from two causes : one, an inspection of only a small part of the walls that were then sealed ; the other, from perhaps not knowing the Saxon method of building in this particular. There are, indeed, intervals of straight-jointing in the square tower, but the Saxon method was not always to bond continuously, but at intervals ; and on sealing the whole of the lower part of the tower we find this intermediate bonding carried throughout. Besides which, the courses of the stones, foreign to the district, clearly show that the square tower and the nave were built together.

Another error arising from imperfect, and perhaps hitherto impossible investigation, is put forward in his pamphlet, which is, that the herring-bone work is confined to the west end of the church ; whereas, on sealing the south wall of the eastern part of the nave, or what was the chancel proper, I find the same herring-bone work in that part. It is also developed on the inside of the crypt wall. Mr. Roberts also argued for the existence of galleries within the nave, but we have carefully probed and examined the whole area of the nave, and not the slightest traces remain to show the existence of any such galleries. Mr. Roberts is a man of genius, of professional and archæological eminence, and of the greatest industry in exploring the records of the past, but this last supposition of his is an inappropriate application of a general custom to a particular case. A further suggestion of his, that the eastern apse itself was encircled by an ambulatory as well as the crypt, may or may not be true, as no proof can be offered on either side of the question. From the examinations that we have been enabled to make in the course of our work, it is clearly ascertained that the square tower, the whole of the nave, with the destroyed aisles, and their terminals, and the eastern apse, were all built at the same time. Exception has been taken to what are called the buttresses of the apse, as indicating a Norman origin, but it may be clearly shown that what really were but slender pilasters were used by the early Saxons ; the projecting parts below, which constitute the buttresses, are simply an addition of my own, as a substitute for the vaulted roof of the ambulatory, by which the slender shafts and walls of the apse were sustained, it being useless to rebuild the ambulatory itself. We have rebuilt this eastern apse on the wall of the crypt, which has been left entire, and having also two sides of the original polygon remaining, we have carefully preserved it, and carried out the building in accordance with them, so that we are certain of having restored this part of the building, both in mode and measure, to its original state.

In the eastern part of the nave or chancel proper I have discovered an early Saxon clerestory arch in the south wall, the lower part of which has been removed for the insertion of the pointed arch below; also, the rim of part of a Norman arch, beneath the clerestory arch of the east end of the nave on the south side, and within this Norman rim, a pointed arch, with a glory painted on fresco, which no doubt surmounted an image of the Virgin. All will be carefully developed and preserved.

I feel greatly indebted to the landlords and parishioners in general, to the Incorporated and District Church Building Societies, and the whole circle of my neighbours and friends around to a radius of six or seven miles in every direction, for the kind and generous support which they have afforded me in this undertaking, as well as to relatives and dear old personal friends in many and distant parts. My first object—to restore the house of God to a state somewhat worthy of His Majesty and goodness, and to secure ample accommodation for all His worshippers in this place, where order, harmony, and goodwill have long prevailed—is so far accomplished. It would be affectation to deny that the discoveries and developments made by me during my long incumbency (which are something like a material offspring to men), the frequent and continued developments in England and in foreign lands, and especially of late in the Holy Land, confirming all my early views and enunciations respecting this singular building, seem to justify me in the hope that my name will be identified with it through future time. And though this is not my native county, one of its fairest and most eligible parts has afforded me a pleasant residence for the last thirty-three years—a full generation in the history and chronology of man—in my earthly pilgrimage, surrounded by many dear and valuable friends, where all my children have either been born or bred (and in many distant parts have reflected no small credit upon it), and wherein I expect to take my earthly rest in her favoured soil; I should, therefore, be greatly wanting in proper feeling if I did not look with anticipated pleasure to bequeath to this county so singular and noble a monument of our remote ancestors in a suitable condition of development and preservation.

Your faithful Colleague,

CHAS. FRED. WATKINS.

BRIXWORTH, *December 11th*, 1865.

BRIXWORTH CHURCH.

The following is an extract from the Report of the Northamptonshire Archæological and Architectural Society, read at a meeting of the members of that Society, on Monday, the 5th of November, 1866 :—

"Of the churches, the repairs or restoration of which have been completed during the last year, first and foremost in antiquity and interest stands Brixworth. Hardly a church in the whole kingdom has an architectural history extending over a longer period, or containing in its pages stronger marks of the different eras of which it is the record. We have in its construction a large use of Roman material ; Roman brick is employed in the construction of one of the finest early arcades in any of our parish churches. Beneath an arch built of such material, and at such a period, are the remnants of a Norman arch, and again underneath these was a decorated window of the same character as others further eastward. Then we have later work of more than one period, besides the more modern repairs and restorations. By excavating the surrounding ground, foundations have been laid bare, revealing a form of building differing in many ways, nor all of one period, from that which has stood for many generations, and in one important instance furnishing a certain guide to the operations of the present restorer. The great peculiarities of Brixworth

Church have been dwelt on at some length in a paper read before this society some years since by Mr. Poole, and to that interesting paper the committee would refer the inquirer. They now make brief allusion to the many styles of architecture existing here, only for the purpose of impressing upon all church restorers the importance of keeping every ancient feature which marks a period, or tells a tale of bygone days. The feature itself may not be one of great beauty, and it might be replaced by one more pleasing to the eye, or more agreeable to harmonious arrangement. But beauty and order in matters of architecture may be sometimes bought too dearly, and the farther any old period of art is receding from us, the greater the reason for our not exchanging 'old lamps for new.' Your committee believe that great care has been, for the most part, shown in the restoration of Brixworth Church ; that, with one minor exception, in which the restorers somewhat differed from the opinion of the committee, every mark of ancient work has been retained, great pains have been taken to supply as little new work as possible, and wherever any new masonry has been inserted, either because constructionally necessary, or to replace any obviously modern excrescence, the new is carefully distinguished from the old. Your committee's remarks, therefore, on the importance of preserving, when practicable, every record of ancient art, are not meant to apply to Brixworth ; to prove, however, the importance of being guided by this conservative spirit in all dealings with our ancient ecclesiastical monuments, we need only bring before our mind's eye the church of Brixworth as it exists to us now, and compare it with what it would have been, had the architects of the fourteenth century, who inserted several windows and executed some minor works there, swept away the pre-existing church, and substituted a Decorated building of even the best proportions. We should have exchanged a unique page of architectural history for an almost stereotyped form of Decorated church."

[Extracted from the *Northampton Herald* of Nov. 17, 1866.]

TO THE EDITOR OF THE "NORTHAMPTON HERALD."

Vicarage, Brixworth, 14*th* *Nov.*, 1866.

Sir,—I am quite satisfied with the report of the committee of the Architectural Society, as published in your last week's number. It entirely vindicates me from a report which had been industriously spread abroad at the commencement of my labours—that I was about to sacrifice all the antiquities of the church, and to spoil the building. This report extended to our Universities, and, I have no doubt, deprived me of receiving aid from archæological parties, and from all parts of this county, except my immediate neighbourhood, where the facts were easily ascertained and generally known, and where I received, in consequence, a most generous support.

The committee report one instance only in which there has been any difference of opinion between us, and I think it due to the county to state my reasons for not yielding to the suggestion of the sub-committee in allowing the decorated windows in dispute to remain. In the first place, the suggestion came too late, as the plans had passed the ordeal of the Incorporated and Diocesan Societies, the parish vestry, and the ordinary, and the contracts were already signed. This was a sufficient reply, and I stated it as one that would be received as a necessity, and prevent any further jarring of opinions. But had it come earlier, I should still have persisted in removing the window, as I had from the first pledged myself to my chief supporters and subscribers, and to the county and archæological world, to restore the church in the full and proper sense of the word—that is, to bring it back to its original state and design, as far as possible—well knowing that I could exhibit and preserve to the county a noble and unique specimen of ecclesiastical architecture, a proud monument of our Saxon fore-fathers, and a connecting link with the earliest religious and

civil buildings of which we have any account, either in sacred
or profane history. [I hope to show this connexion, and its
important bearing upon civil and religious uses, in a forth-
coming treatise on the Basilica, of which there is no satisfactory history in any language, together with a complete
history of Brixworth Church, with suitable lithographs.] I
could not, therefore, allow a bad specimen of a much later date,
as this window was, to mar the consistency and harmony of
what the committee justly style "one of the finest early arcades
in any of our parish churches." The ruinous state of the wall
which the Gothic insertors left around it alone would have
rendered it necessary to remove it, and the retention of a better
window of the period in another part of the church, where it is
less injurious, should reconcile any one to the removal of this.

I am thankful to say that I have been spared to complete
this undertaking far beyond my first expectations, at an outlay
of about 2500l. ; that all the expenses have been paid as they
were incurred ; that an obligation for the balance of 200l. still
required has been partly met by a gentleman who has no permanent interest in the county, and who has already contributed
150l., by offering to give 50l. more, if the remaining 150l. be
subscribed.

Yours, &c.,

C. F. WATKINS.

P.S.—It is gratifying to me to record that, a fortnight before
his accident, my old friend Dr. Whewell came to see my
restorations, in company with Mackworth Dolben, Esq., and
expressed his approbation to him and me of all that I had
done.

RESTORATIONS.

With respect to the principles involved in the repairs and restitutions of our churches, I do not think the nature of the style in the architecture of so much consequence, except so far as one may conduce more than another to deeper and more solemn impressions in Divine worship; nor have I any prejudice against the Greco-Italian churches of Sir Christopher Wren.

The great merit of repairing and restoring our churches consists in this—that it produces and maintains a greater reverence for the Supreme Being and sacred things, and raises the tone of religious and moral sentiments. For how can man, if duly impressed with feelings of reverence for his Maker, and for things pertaining to His worship, contentedly enter from time to time into His consecrated dwelling, and see it with composure falling into decay, or presenting a meaner appearance than his own stables, whilst he himself has just come out of chambers adorned with "cedar and vermilion?" If it be a question whether the want of reverence and religious feeling on the one hand, or the former state of our churches on the other, be the cause or effect, they are very certainly correlative and reciprocal.

One of the great difficulties was a very wide suspicion and fear of its being a movement in favour of Popery. And this, though utterly unfounded with respect to the persons concerned, was nevertheless in itself a holy and patriotic jealousy, excited by the extreme practices of indiscreet zealots, as well as perverts, and fanned, even to the present moment, by the unworthy insinuations of many whose views of sacred matters are as low as their actions are mean and despicable.

It would indeed be a sad disgrace to us if we conceded to the Romanist, to the Mahometan, and the heathen, the exclusive performance of the duty, and the sole exercise of the privilege of bringing the first-fruits, the best and choicest of material things, to adorn and beautify the Palace of the "Great King of all the Earth ;" and we, who profess a purer and more favoured religion, should return Him nothing of the greater riches which He has bestowed upon us, but the dregs and refuse of our abundant stores! A Mahometan coming to this country, and seeing the marvellous structures erected within the last quarter of a century for the purposes of commerce, manufactures, art, and domestic enjoyment—their magnitude, costliness, and ornamentation ; and knowing the dilapidated and unsightly state of most of our churches at the commencement of that period, would necessarily exclaim, "This is a people that worship the creature more than the Creator ;" "They are votaries of Mammon."

With regard to the re-seating of our churches, nothing could be more obstructive to the true spirit of Christianity, and to an acceptable worship of the Father of our Lord Jesus Christ, than the elevated or secluded pews which have hitherto encroached upon the areas of our churches, in fostering self-indulgence, listlessness, and both worldly and spiritual pride. But now, where the seats are open and level, and accommodation made for the poorer members of the parochial family, the humblest individual may "enter the courts of the Lord with joy," and say to himself with an honest and grateful exultation, "My Father's House"—"How amiable are Thy dwellings, Thou Lord of Hosts!" He may now feel with complacency that he is acknowledged by the rich and noble to be one of the children of the same common Father and Lord of all, a brother in Christ, and a fellow-heir of the same heavenly kingdom ; whilst the upper classes are hereby reminded that eventually "the rich and poor will meet together," without respect of persons, in the immediate presence of their Maker, and that the talents

entrusted to their care are soon to be withdrawn and accounted
for ; and, instead of allowing the clerk to act a vicarial part for
them in the response and acts of devotion, all are hereby in-
fluenced to personal and united worship, and " with one mind
and one mouth to glorify their Maker." Thus sympathy and
care will be exercised by the latter on behalf of the humbler
members of Christ's body, whilst a true feeling of respect and
attachment will be engendered in these towards the upper
classes. And thus the different classes of society will be united
together by the strongest of all bonds, and be enabled to meet
and overcome all dangers that may threaten from without, and
all the severest trials which can happen within the kingdom.
It is satisfactory to find that the highest and oldest of our
nobility and gentry are the most ready to relinquish class dis-
tinctions in Divine worship, as their longer residence and
sympathies with their humbler brethren might lead us to
expect.

C. F. W.

HISTORY OF THE CHURCH.

THE time when this church was erected is certified to us by Leland, on the authority of Hugo, the Monk of Peterborough, as having taken place under the rule of the Abbot Saxulphus or Sexwulf of Peterborough, then called Medhamsted, towards the latter end of the seventh century.

The particular year is uncertain; but about 690 it was a dependency of Medhamsted, and accompanied with a monastery, some remains of which were lately discovered by the present Vicar on rebuilding the vicarage-house, consisting of a Saxon arch which fell down with an old wall, and of a transition arch, as well as in the exhumation of decayed coffins and skeletons.

This testimony of Hugo is confirmed by successive alterations of an architectural character, which can be traced in a retrograde order, from the time of Henry VI., through the Decorated,

the Early English, the Post-Norman transition,
the late Norman and the late Saxon, the most
ancient and conclusive of which is the round
tower appended to the square porch at the west
end, loopholed all round for archery, with a wind-
ing staircase from top to bottom,—most probably
to serve for defence against the incursion of the
Danes; and coeval with this a three-light window
with baluster shafts, like those at Earl's Barton,
and St. Bennet's, Cambridge, set in upon an
earlier semicircular arch of the same character
as the rest of the original structure, the crown of
which was cut away to receive that three-light
window.

The original aisles, too, which were built and
bonded in with the arcade, having the piers of
their transverse arches locked in between those of
the nave, must have been destroyed before the
Norman period, for a Norman doorway has been
inserted—for an entrance—in one of the original
arches of the nave, which could not have been
done had the south aisle been standing. And
this confirms the account given by Tanner in his
"Notitia," of the aisles having been destroyed by
the Danes in 870, and of the round tower having
been appended soon after that time to secure the

church, and perhaps the inhabitants, against any future injury from those fierce invaders.

Thus we deduce the erection of the main structure, consisting of the nave, the square tower, the remains of the eastern apse, the destroyed aisles with their double terminals (which I shall hereafter show to be all of the same date), to precede the ninth century, when the alterations first commenced, and therefore corroborate the story of Hugo the Monk.

NAMES OF THE PLACE.

In the Saxon Chronicle, the name of the place is written Bricklesworthe; in Domesday, Briclesworde, but no mention is made therein of the Church. The next intelligence is of the value of the living,—in Pope Nicholas' taxation 21*l.* 6*s.* 8*d.* for the Rectory, and 4*l.* 13*s.* 4*d.* for the Vicarage, where the name is written Briklesworthe, and afterwards Brikelsworth. The present name is first found in the "Valor Ecclesiasticus." The original word Bricklesworthe, according to Bridges, denotes its fame for springs; and truly in a lordship of more than 3000 acres there is scarce a field in which you cannot arrive at a spring of moderate depth, and generally one near the surface, which vindicates the auspicious meaning of the word. In this last dry summer (1865) we had no failure of its springs.

Bridges supposes the Rectory to have been given soon *after the Conquest* (Mr. Lear, Precentor of Salisbury Cathedral and Prebendary of Brixworth, tells me "in the thirteenth century;" and this agrees with the History which Bridges himself gives of the Successive Prebendaries and Vicars, as commencing only from that time) to Salisbury Cathedral, the Chancellor of the Cathedral Church there holding it as his Prebend till the death of the late Prebendary, the Hon. Hugh Percy, Bishop of Carlisle, at whose decease it was transferred to the Ecclesiastical Commissioners, who sold the Prebendal Estate to Lord Overstone, compensating the lessee, the Rev. W. W. Hume, for his interest in three lives; and the Vicarage which was formed out of the rectorial property at its translation to the Chancellorship of Salisbury Cathedral, and in his patronage, was vested in the Bishop of Peterborough when the prebendal land was sold.

Having given this general sketch of the origin of the church, and its relative dependency, I shall now enter into full particulars respecting its original

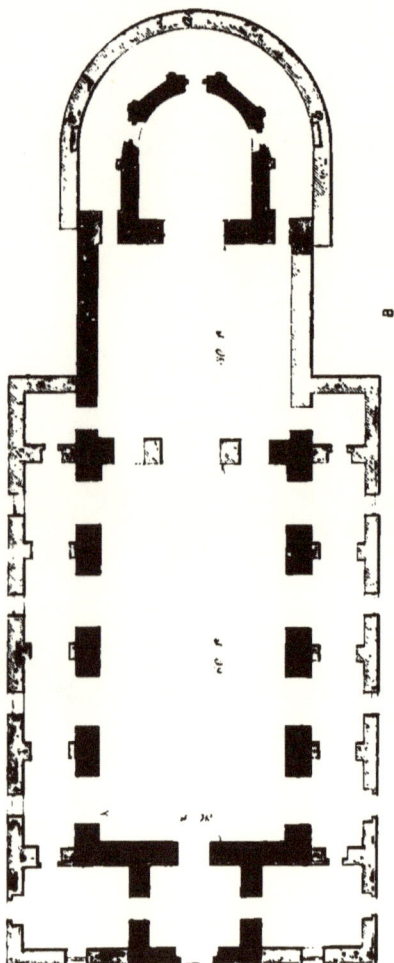

ORIGINAL GROUND PLAN

Scale of feet

a. Ambulatory Wall
b. Recess

█ Dark tint indicates existing remains of original Building

▨ Light tint indicates part of original Building supposed to have been destroyed by the Danes in 871

A Saxon Staircase & Turret supposed to have been built about AD 670

B Mortuary Chapel about 1075

plan; the materials with which it was built; the nature and purport of the successive alterations, and the manner in which it is being restored.

The ground-plan annexed, and taken from existing remains, shows that it was built after the earliest types of the Basilica, traced through Roman examples to one in Nineveh discovered by Layard : viz., a nave divided into two parts of one and two thirds, of thirty and sixty feet respectively in length, and of the width of thirty feet throughout, as in the earliest examples given by me in the History of the Basilica. A square porch at the west of the nave, and recessed from the outer wall of the nave on either side to the extent of nine feet.

An eastern apse, polygonal without, and semicircular within, surrounded by a corridor or ambulatory, the outward wall of which is parallel to the inner circular wall; having recesses in some of the sides, and receiving a vaulted ceiling from the string course of the inner circular wall). Contrary to expectation, I found the original floor of the chancel on a level with that of the church, and unbroken ground beneath : so that there could have been no crypt under the church, but only the ambulatory around it and beneath. North and south aisles, each terminating at the east end in a square apse; and at the west end in an oblong, the recess from the wall of the nave to the square tower being added to the square terminal of the aisle.

The whole nave is ninety feet long by thirty in width, originally parted at two-thirds its length, or sixty feet, from its west end by a transverse wall—now no more—with a central or triumphal arch in the middle, corresponding to the large arch which leads into the eastern apse. Besides this central arch, the bases of whose piers I developed by excavation some years ago, it had arched openings on either side with clear story windows above, corresponding and opposite to those at the east end.

The walls of the nave between the west end and the extinct partition—sixty feet in length—consist, on either side, of four bays, the arches semi-circular, built with Roman tiles, or flat bricks of large dimensions, mostly in two courses, resting upon square imposts of the same material, set upon square piers of brick tiles and stone intermixed, *more Romano*. Above, on either side, are three clerestory windows, built in the same form, but much narrower and smaller, not immediately

NAVE LOOKING EAST

SOUTH AISLE EAST

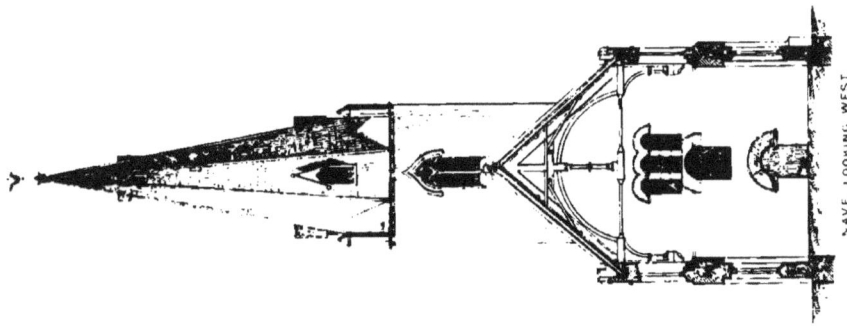

NAVE LOOKING WEST

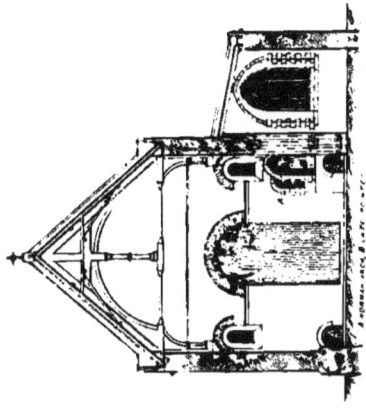

over the lower arches, but in the perpendicular between each two. They are constructed with a mixture of stone and fragments of bricks, as though all the whole bricks taken from a previous building had been exhausted in the construction of the lower arches, and none but these fragments remained to intermix with stone in the clerestory formation.

That the Roman tiles used in this church were taken from a pre-existing Roman building is evident, not only from their fragmentary character in the clerestory, and even in the piers and walls beneath, but also from the appearance of Roman mortar, of a different character from the rest, still adhering, and manifest some time ago, to one of the tiles; but now, I regret to say, pointed over by churchwardens' over-careful direction.

It is a reasonable presumption that the Romans had a station here of some importance, as there is a castrametation in the paddock adjoining the churchyard, and it is central in the line of the forts which have been traced on either side, from the Wash on the east to the Severn on the west of the island; and Roman coins of Antoninus Pius and Carausius, and Roman urns have been dug up in the place. The reasonable conclusion

is that the Saxons of the 7th century rebuilt after
the form of a provincial Basilica, or stationary
Pretorium of the earliest and simplest type. Since
this was written I discovered within the square
tower the bases of circular columns which formed
the propyleum to the Roman temple, or early
Christian Church, after which this was built. I also
discovered in one of the piers of the early Saxon
arches a Roman eagle of the Assyrian type, built in
by the Saxons, and evidently taken from an earlier
building, as having mortices in which some standard
had been fixed.

I at one time supposed that the clerestory was
of a later date than the arcade beneath—that it
had been either rebuilt or superimposed; and I
regret having, I fear, misled Professor Willis to
misconceive the dates. But now that the walls
are scaled throughout the interior, I find them to
have been built at the same time.

The materials used, besides the Roman tiles,
were principally the stones of the neighbouring
beds, which belong to the lias formation. These
beds consist of three courses, the upper a thin
schale of calcareous and siliceous mixture, used
principally in building dry walls and draining;
the lower a thick sandy stone, impregnated more

or less with iron, and at the lowest part of a blue and more calcareous character, hardening more and more as it is exposed to evaporation, yielding, though with difficulty, at its first coming out to the chisel, but not capable of a level surface, or of being finely jointed. The intermediate course is highly ferruginous; and for the most part perishes either with wet or frost, though some pieces are sufficiently weather-proof to be used in rubble masonry. And the masonry of this church is, for the most part, of a rubbly texture, strengthened at the corners with large rude blocks of granite, sandstone, and clay slate, transported from other strata; and, as well as the rubbly stones, cemented together by a mortar as hardened as the stones themselves. There is also a kind of tufa or carbonate of lime used in the upper arch of the square tower, but very sparsely mixed in this local bed.

The lower walls are four feet thick, the clerestory narrowing from a set-off on either side by several inches.

The square tower is of the same massive character as the nave, with similar arches on its four sides—the largest to the west forming the original grand entrance to the building; a lesser one leading into the nave; and, on the sides, two

still smaller ones, leading into the western terminals, or apsidal chambers of the north and south
aisles. Mr. Roberts contends for a later period to
this porch than that of the nave, from some
straight jointing which he perceived; but on
scaling the walls this is found to be but partial,
and in consequence of some alterations in the
original work. This running up straight joints,
and bonding at intervals only, appears to be a
Saxon mode, and answers to their method of bind-
ing by wooden frames. Not only is the square
tower bonded in with the nave, though at intervals,
but the several diverse materials are worked up
line for line in the one and in the other. The
arches, too, are similar in their form and material,
composed of Roman tiles as entire as those of the
nave; whereas, if the tower had been of a later
date, there would not have been any whole tiles
left for the construction of the arches: they would
have had only fragments of tiles, like those remaining in the clerestory. Moreover, the square
tower was subject to the first alterations of which
we have any evidence, that is in the year 870.
For when the round tower was then, or soon
after, appended thereto, and pierced for archery,
to protect the place against any fresh aggression

of the Danes, the semicircular arch in the east end of the square tower was shorn of its crown, to receive the three-light window with baluster shafts, as a substitute for the window in the west end, which had been closed up by the building of the round tower; and the grand west entrance of the square tower was, at the same time, filled in, with the exception of a space for a smaller arch of entrance into the round tower, included within the greater arch.

The north and south aisles, with their terminal chambers, were also of the same date as the nave, having their piers locked into the walls of the nave, between the piers of the nave arches.

The eastern apse also was of the same date and style, with a string course of Roman bricks on the wall of the crypt, upon which the apse itself rested, and from which the vaulting of the ambulatory sprang: this vaulted roofing resting on a low outer wall built to receive it.

The appearance of buttresses to this apse has led some archæologists to suppose it a Norman structure; but Sir Gardiner Wilkinson has shown that slight shafts pertained to the Saxon period, and the buttresses beneath were placed by me as a substitute for the vaulting to support the walls above.

The next alteration that took place after the appendage of the round tower, and the insertion of the three-light baluster shafted window in the east end of the square tower, was the introduction of a late Norman doorway in the first arch of the nave on the south side, reckoning from the west, which infers the destruction of the south aisle before this period. I was at a loss to determine where this doorway could come from, till on scaling the wall at the east end of the church I found part of the rim of a late Norman arch, and a wall of the same period, forming part of a chapel, preceding the present Early English aisle ; and hence, no doubt, on the supersession of this chapel, came this door to the other end. Then followed the insertion of a transition arch in the next bay to this, the upper part of which I have preserved to view : for I think it right to preserve one specimen of each style that has been introduced up to the latest period.

The present south aisle was next added in the Early English period, as a chapel for the family of Sir John de Verdun, Lord of the Manor, whose effigy I have just rescued from the barbarous treatment to which it had been subjected by being removed from its horizontal bed, and violently thrust with his legs into the ground so as to break them off, and the head into the wall of the arched recess in which it was first laid.

For access to this chapel, the smaller arch at the east end was cut out of the south wall of the choir; and about fifty years afterwards the larger arch was opened, the difference in the dates being evinced by the style of each. A small window also was inserted above in the same wall of the choir. Above the earliest of these arches I have laid open a Saxon clerestory arch, the lower part of which was cut away to receive the pointed one beneath. It would be about the same period in which this larger arch was made that the partition wall between the nave and choir, with its central triumphal arch, its side openings below, and clerestory windows above, all corresponding to those at the east end of the choir, was removed, and the present wide arch inserted to span the whole width of the nave and choir.

Then followed the insertion of three decorated windows, one under the transition window in the second bay of the nave on the south side; one in the third bay on the north side, and one at the west end of the choir on the same side. This last is preserved: the two former are removed as in-

E

terfering with the restoration of the Saxon arcade, the one in the choir being sufficient to show the progress of alteration which the building has undergone by successive innovations. The decorated window to the east of this in the same wall of the choir is only of twenty years' date, substituted at the rebuilding of that part of the wall, then in ruin, for a miserable little nondescript of a square form, which had been thrust into the wall at some late period.

Then succeeded the insertion of two wretched windows of the perpendicular kind, one on either side of the nave, which have been removed from the arches in which they had been intruded to the regret of no one, and the joy of many.

In the reign of Henry VI., the chancel must have been elongated, as the late east window would testify. Whether the original apse had remained entire up to this period, or had undergone previous mutilation, it is impossible to say. Luckily two sides of the outward polygon, with the outward parallel wall, and the corresponding part of the ambulatory, two recesses, and the original steps of descent remain, and the whole circular wall of the crypt upon which the apse was built; so as to direct us rightly in the restoration

of this interesting portion of the original
building.

I have only to remark on the eastern wall of the
nave or choir, that the noble central arch therein
remains entire as originally built : but at the insertion of the screen the original piers were taken
out to widen the entrance into the chancel, and
wooden uprights and cross pieces substituted.
When I came to reside I found the uprights
decaying at the ground, and all in danger of
falling. As soon as possible I removed these
wooden props, and substituted brick piers, and
had the satisfaction of finding the bases of the
original piers, on which I erected their present
successors.

The two clerestory windows above are developed
in the eastern wall which served to throw light
into the choir ; and two similar clerestory windows
in the opposite wall brought a further portion of
light into that part of the church from the clerestory of the nave.

Underneath these clerestory windows were
arched doorways, those at the east end leading
down to the ambulatory, and at the west end into
the choir from the nave.

The only monuments of any interest to the

antiquary, in this church, are, a stone slab, with an inscription in Norman French, early in the 14th century, to the memory of Adam de Taunton, vicar of the parish.

A similar one to the memory of Simon Curteis, of the same period.

The brasses have been removed from both, and the inscriptions, preserved in Bridges' History of the County, are wearing out.

Another of the same kind and period, only partially decipherable, and I think to one Hugo— Query the Monk ?

These three are in the floor of the nave.

An effigy of a Knight Templar—probably Sir John de Verdun—in an arched recess.

A late altar-tomb to Lord Invernry in a similar arched recess. These two are in the south aisle. There is in the south aisle also a handsome oak screen of the 16th century.

The market-cross has long been removed from the base which still remains; and I have the upright shaft in which I think it was fixed—there are Saxon ornaments upon this shaft.

REOPENING OF BRIXWORTH CHURCH.

This venerable church, which has an historical authority, in the testimony of Hugo the Monk, as recorded by Dugdale in his "Monasticon," for its origin in the latter part of the 7th century, and this testimony well corroborated by a succession of every style of architecture since imposed upon the building—the Later Saxon, Norman, Transition, Early English, Decorated, and Tudor—was on Wednesday, the 11th July, 1866, reopened, after a thorough restoration: 247 additional free seats have also hereby been secured.

The principal contributors have been Earl Spencer, Sir Charles Isham, Thomas Wood, Esq., of Brixworth Hall; Joceline Watkins, Esq., of Calcutta; and the Incorporated and Diocesan Church Building Societies. Special gifts for memorials and other purposes have been made or promised by the Earl of Kintore, General Lawrenson, and the surviving officers of the 14th Light Dragoons, to the memory of Lord Inverury; Sir C. and Lady Isham, Charles Morris, Esq., Messrs. A. B. Markham, W. Shaw, of Cotton-end; W. Roberts, of Albion-place; Joceline Watkins, and the rest of the Vicar's family; and Messrs. Minton, Hollins, and Co. (whose beautiful encaustic tiles, generously presented by them for the floor of the chancel, were exceedingly admired). Very handsome kneeling cushions were worked by the Brixworth ladies for the Communion service, and two richly worked stools presented by Mrs. Attenborough, of Brampton Ash.

The day for the opening was every thing that could be
desired, and from 500 to 600 persons were present at either
service. The preacher for the morning was the Rev. E.
Trollope ; for the afternoon, the Rev. T. Yard—both accomplished antiquaries and able divines. Their discourses were
suitable and excellent, but that of Mr. Yard was imperfectly
heard, and he did not appear in good health; otherwise he is
both audible and admirable in his discourses. The prayers
were read by the Vicar, assisted by the Rev. H. James, Rev.
R. Isham, Rev. G. H. Vyse, Rev. G. A. Poole, and the Hon.
and Rev. A. G. Douglas, in reading the Litany and the Lessons.
The blessing was given by the Vicar. The two collections
amounted to 94l. The parishioners conceded the occupation of
the seats to the public on this occasion.

After the morning service about 200 of the gentry and clergy
retired to the vicarage, and partook of refreshments under an
awning on the lawn.—Sir C. Isham proposed the health of the
Vicar, and spoke of the restoration as all that could be wished.
—Mr. Watkins replied to the compliment with expressions of
grateful acknowledgment to the gentry, clergy, and others of
the neighbourhood, who had so kindly and generously assisted
him in the work ; and particularly for the encouragement he met
with from Earl Spencer, his constant friends Sir C. and Lady
Isham, Mr. Wood, and his son in India, and concluded with
proposing the health of Messrs. Trollope and Yard.—After the
second service about 100 of the congregation partook of tea
and other refreshments at the vicarage ; and in the evening the
choir and others engaged about the church were entertained
there to a supper. The principal inhabitants opened their
houses and spread their tables with hospitable entertainment to
numerous friends and visitors ; and altogether the day passed
over without default of any kind. The restoration reflects the
highest credit upon the care and ability of Messrs. Slater and
Smith, the architects, who have most assiduously, and with a
real love of their art, carried out the desires of the Vicar. Mr.

Thompson, the clerk of the works, has also shown himself thoroughly acquainted with the principles as well as the technicalities of his art. Mr. Trollope kindly took the company round the church between and after the conclusion of the services, and gave them an instructive lecture upon the building. Amongst the company we noticed Sir C. and Lady Isham and daughters, Sir C. Rous Boughton, Bart., and Lady Boughton, A. Boughton Knight, Esq., and Mrs. B. Knight, J. and H. Nethercote, Esqrs., and the ladies of the family ; — Orlebar, Esq., and Mrs. Orlebar, Capt. and Mrs. Stockdale, James Barry, Esq., Mayor of Northampton ; the Revs. G. H. Vyse, R. Isham, the Hon. G. A. Douglas, A. Bromhead, Hitchens, Montgomery, Poole, Sutton, Sanders, Dr. Gifford, T. C. Thornton, F. C. Alderson, Monkhouse, Houseman, Thos. Bull, Dalton, Rokeby, Roberts, J. Field, Parker, Lawson, Cookson, Casson, Day, Bailey, Harper, Knight, Evans, Newby, Clayton, Burnaby, &c., with ladies and children ; Messrs. Terry, T. Scriven, T. Butlin, &c.

—

SPECIAL HYMNS,

Composed by the Rev. C. F. Watkins, for the Reopening of Brixworth Church.

MORNING SERVICE.

PROCESSIONAL HYMN.

O Thou ! who art enthroned above,
Where myriads serve with zeal and love,
 Look down on this our festal day ;
While songs of joy, and hymns of praise
To Thee in grateful strains we raise,
 And for Thy Blessing humbly pray.

Behold the portals, opened wide,
Invite within the flowing tide
  Of eager votaries, hastening past
To meet within this ancient fane,
Worthy to be Thy House again,
  And for Thy Service meet at last.

Do Thou a gracious hearing lend,
While every voice is tuned to blend
  Devotion framed in harmony:
Within their Common Father's hall,
Noble and gentle, great and small,
  United wait to worship Thee.

If we this new-raised temple mourn
Of pristine glory robbed and shorn,
  Do Thou a greater lustre shed
By coming now within her gates,
That every soul on Thee that waits
  To Thy Salvation may be led.   Amen.

INVOCATIONAL HYMN.

Great God! who from Eternity's dark womb
  Didst birth and progress upon Time bestow,
And bade it all material things consume
  By the strong action of its ceaseless flow:

In favour Thou didst graciously ordain
  That on these walls his course should lightly press,
Twelve centuries spare this aged hallowed fane,
  Respecting still where Thou still deign'st to bless.

While we each outward waste of time repair,
  And, what man's hand had marred, will skill restore,
Do Thou our inward souls preserve with care,
  Our hearts renew, and strengthen more and more:

That when this house of stone, and ours of clay,
    At length, by Time, in earth and dust are laid,
We thence may rise to where there's no decay,
    And purer worship ever shall be made. Amen.

ADMONITORY HYMN.

Within this consecrated fane
    The voice of God and Nature hear!
With you they plead, and plead again
    From age to age, from year to year.

Near forty generations, gone,
    Unto her holy font were brought,
God's own adopted made anon,
    Whom Christ's own precious blood had bought.

Near forty generations, too,
    Before the Altar here have gained
His Blessing—sure to all who woo
    For that sweet love which He ordained.

And all of that once infant race,
    And all of those thus wedded pairs
Were brought again within this place
    Beyond their own and others' prayers.

The thousand and two hundred years
    Like yesterday have passed and fled,
Nor of those races one appears;
    But all are vanished, all are dead!

Within and round about us lie
    Their bones and dust which, year by year,
Still raise the soil, till, rising high,
    And higher still the mounds appear.

But where are now the spirits found
   That once informed those heaps of clay?
They are not in that rising ground,
   But far in other worlds away.

They who were deaf to God's blest word,
   And Nature's urgent plea refused,
In wailing misery now are heard,
   And warn of mercies long abused.

And they who here were timely wise,
   And listened, and in faith obeyed,
Are now in that sweet Paradise
   Which Christ hath for His people made.

And we are hastening, like them all,
   To join their dust and spirits too;
Then list to God and Nature's call—
   The road the wise have gone pursue.   Amen.

EVENING SERVICE.

INTRODUCTORY HYMN.

The gracious mandate hear!
It issues from above:
The Bridegroom's voice is loud and clear,
   And calls to thee in love.

Arise! and shine again!
Thy faded garb renew!
Rub off the rust, wash out the stain!
   Assume a brighter hue!

No more in dust to lie
With garment soiled and torn,
To grieve the stranger passing by
   And bid thy children mourn.

An aged mother now —
In youth of beauty rare—
Right grand in form and face wert thou,
With every feature fair.

And though of some bereft,
Thy stately form remains,
And thou in Queen-like guise art left
And reverence still pertains.

Now all thy children bring!
To God their voices raise!
This day the Bridegroom and the King
Should hear their joy and praise. Amen.

THE HOLY CATHOLIC CHURCH.

O Thou! who camest on earth to save,
And built Thy Church to stem the wave;
Through tempest, storm, and time t'endure,
Her strong foundations laid so sure.

See! beauteous stones by Prophets brought,
More beauteous still the Apostles wrought;
That all the building raised on high
Secure might rest, and force defy.

Thy holy Word effulgence pours,
And lighteneth all within her doors:
From earliest dawn inspired, and still
With clearer rays, to show Thy will,

Till latest inspiration given,
It opens wide the view of heaven,
And leaves no mist to dull the sight
Of blissful hope and glory bright:

Thine own commissioned Pastors there
Thy people lead in humble prayer;
And teach their tongues on high to raise
The grateful strains of thanks and praise.   Amen.

Second Part.

With promised pardon, firmly sealed,
By the blest sign to man revealed
Of that which bore Thy bleeding frame,
They give Thy children place and name,

And lead them on, from day to day,
Beneath that banner, to the fray,
Till fuller grace and greater strength
Are, with Thy presence, gained at length,

Where Thou dost of Thyself impart
A share to every faithful heart,
That those who here for Thee would die
Conjoined with Thee, might reign on high.

O blest communion, firm and sure
To him who eats in faith, secure—
Secure of grace and bliss divine—
So rich is this repast of Thine.

The strongest walls on earth will shake,
Whene'er the earth may rock and quake,
And human hands that build the wall
May cause its stones to rend and fall.

But none this Heaven-built house can shock,
So built—so founded on the rock :
Wide as the world, and unconfined
To hold and shelter all mankind.   Amen.

SUBSCRIBERS

TO

THE RESTORATION OF BRIXWORTH CHURCH.

	£	s.	d.
Andrew, Rev. W. W. .	30	0	0
Attenborough, Mrs., and the Misses Weston .	30	0	0
Architects, the. . . .	10	0	0
Attenborough, Jas. Esq. .	5	0	0
Adnitt, Messrs. J. and S.	5	0	0
Argles, Rev. Canon . .	5	0	0
Annand, Mrs.	1	0	0
Ayres, Mr.	2	2	0
Atterbury, Mr. H. . .	1	0	0
Archer, Mr.	1	1	0
Archer, Miss	0	5	0
Abel, Mr.	1	1	0
Allen, Mr. Thos. . . .	2	2	0
Bishop, the late . . .	20	0	0
Bishop, the	10	0	0
Brawn, Mr.	15	0	0
Bateman, Lord . . .	10	0	0
Bevan, R. L. Esq. . .	60	0	0
Beynon, Rev. E. F. . .	5	0	0
Burghley, Lord . . .	5	0	0
Bigge, Rev. H. . . .	1	0	0
Bouverie, General .	5	0	0
Blencowe, J. Esq. . .	3	3	0
Barkell, Mrs. (cards) .	2	2	0
Butlin, Mr. W. . . .	2	2	0
Butlin, Rev. W. . . .	5	0	0
Boyd, Captain	2	0	0
Bull, two Misses . . .	5	0	0
Bromhead, Rev. A. . .	2	0	0
Biddles, Jacob, Esq. . .	5	0	0
Barber, Mr., Hannington	1	0	0
Barber, Mr., Moulton .	1	0	0
Birch, Rev. F. . . .	2	0	0
Bates, Mrs.	2	2	0

	£	s.	d.
Church Building Society, Incorporated . . .	150	0	0
Ditto, Diocesan . .	100	0	0
Cave, Lewis, Esq. . . .	10	0	0
Cave, Mrs. L.	10	0	0
Cox, Rev. R. H. . . .	2	2	0
Compton, Lord Alwyn .	2	0	0
Cleaver, Mr. and Mrs. .	2	2	0
Couchman, Rev. J. . .	5	0	0
Clarke, Mr. G. . . .	3	0	0
Concert, 1st	9	12	0
Concert, 2nd	16	7	9
Crawley, Rev. H. . . .	5	0	0
Crawley, Miss Susan . .	2	0	0
Crowe, Rev. E. . . .	5	0	0
Callis, Mrs. J.	5	0	0
Curtis, Mr.	1	0	0
Carpet, Old	1	0	0
Casson, Rev. G. . . .	3	3	0
Concert, 3rd	3	0	0
Commercial Traveller .	0	5	0
Douglas, Hon. and Rev. G. A.	5	0	0
Durant, Captain . . .	5	0	0
Dolben, Mackworth, Esq.	5	0	0
Dickenson, Mrs. . . .	1	1	0
Dennis, Mr.	1	1	0
Davys, Archdeacon . .	5	0	0
Davis, Rev. J.	1	1	0
Davis, H. Esq. . . .	1	1	0
Digby, G. O. W. Esq. .	5	0	0
Day, Mr., Old	2	0	0
Davis, Mrs.	0	5	0
Elworthy, Mr.	20	0	0

	£	s.	d.		£	s.	d.
Eady, Mr. F.	1	0	0	Ireland, Mr.	3	0	0
Faux, J. Esq.	5	0	0	Judge, Spencer, Esq. .	1	1	0
Flood, Mr.	2	0	0	Jones, Rev. Jonathan .	1	11	6
Fisher, E. K. Esq. . .	2	2	0	Jones. Mr.	1	1	0
Fitzhugh, Mr.	5	0	0	Jeyes, P. Esq.. . . .	1	0	0
Fife, Captain	1	0	0	Jeyes, Mr. Frank . . .	3	0	0
Friend, A	2	0	0	James, Miss	1	0	0
Field, Rev. J.	1	1	0	Knightley, R. Esq., M.P.	5	0	0
Field, Rev. J. jun. . .	0	10	6	Kingsdown, Lord . . .	10	0	0
Glasgow, Earl of . . .	25	0	0	Kintore, Earl of . . .	10	10	0
Green, Miss	15	0	0	Kinsey, Miss	2	2	0
Goode, Messrs. . . .	15	0	0	Knight, Rev. R. . . .	1	0	0
Goode, Mr. E.. . . .	2	0	0	Knight, Rev. J. . . .	2	0	0
Glover, Rev. J. H. . .	1	1	0	Locock, the Family . .	68	0	0
Gaylor, Mr.	2	2	0	Lowe, —, Esq., Calcutta	10	0	0
Gall, Rev. F. H. . . .	2	0	0	Langham, Herbert, Esq.	10	0	0
Goodday, Rev. S.. . .	0	10	0	Lawrenson, General, and			
Gage, Mr. S.	3	0	0	Officers of 14th Lan-			
Gates, Brook, Esq. . .	1	1	0	cers	21	0	0
Grant, W. Esq. . . .	2	2	0	Lamport Charity Land .	15	0	0
Gubbings, Ann . . .	0	0	6	Lindsay, Spencer, Esq..	1	0	0
Gray, Mr., Courtenhall .	1	0	0	Lovell, Isaac, Esq. . .	2	0	0
Goodday, A. Esq.. . .	1	0	0	Lovell, Isaac Edward,			
Harper, F. L. Esq. . .	10	0	0	Esq.	2	0	0
Hewitt, Henry, Esq.. .	5	0	0	Lovell, Thos. Esq. . .	1	1	0
Higgins, Messrs. J. K. .	2	2	0	Lear, Rev. F.	1	0	0
Higgins, W.	2	2	0	Lynes, G. B. Esq. . .	1	0	0
Higgins, H.	2	2	0	Markham, the Misses,			
Herrick,Mrs.,Beaumanor	10	0	0	Bessel Green, Kent .	8	0	0
Hope, A. Beresford, Esq.	5	0	0	Markham, E. Esq., Lon-			
Harrison, W. Esq. . .	1	0	0	don	1	0	0
Howard, —, Esq.. . .	1	0	0	Markham, Arthur, Esq..	6	0	0
Hoey, Mr.	1	0	0	Markham, Henry, Esq..	1	0	0
Huntsman, Mrs. . . .	2	2	0	Marriot, G. P. Esq. . .	3	13	6
Hanbury. —, Esq. . .	1	0	0	Montgomery, Rev. R. .	5	0	0
Howes, J. Esq. . . .	1	0	0	Montgomery, Wm. Esq.	3	0	0
Hill, Mr., Commercial .	0	5	0	Morris, Charles, Esq. .	10	0	0
Isham, Sir Chas. Bart. .	150	0	0	Morris, the Misses . .		0	0
Isham, Lady	15	0	0	Nethercote, J. Esq. . .	5	0	0
Isham, Dowager Lady .	5	0	0	Nethercote, H. O. Esq..	10	0	0
Irby, Hon. and Rev. P.A.	5	5	0	Overstone, Lord . . .	200	0	0
Irby, Hon. Mrs. . . .	1	1	0	Offertory, the			
Irby, Rev. G.	3	0	0	Osborne, Thos. Esq.. .	5	0	0
Isham, Rev. R. . . .	5	0	0	Opening, the	103	0	0
Interest	6	1	0	Parker, Rev. F. . . .	5	0	0
Ditto	4	3	0				
Ditto	1	19	0				

	£	s.	d.
Pell, Albert, Esq.. . .	3	0	0
Phipps and Son, Messrs.			
J.	2	2	0
Phipps, Pickering, Esq. .	2	2	0
Pickering, Mr. J. . . .	3	0	0
Pickering, Mr. B. . . .	3	3	0
Pownall, Rev. J. . . .	1	0	0
Payne, Mr. Chas. . . .	3	0	0
Pell, Mr. S., Ecton Lodge			
Pierce, Mr. J. W. . .	1	1	0
Robarts, A. R. Esq., M.P.	5	0	0
Randolph, Admiral . .	5	0	0
Robarts, Mrs.	5	0	0
Revis, J. Esq.	1	0	0
Reeve, Mr., Guilsborough	0	10	3
Spencer, Earl, K.G. . .	100	0	0
Shaw, W. Esq., Cotton			
End	10	0	0
Scrimgeour, J. Esq. . .	10	0	0
Seymour, E. W. Esq. .	10	0	0
Smith, Mr. J. U. . . .	6	6	0
Sawbridge, Mrs. . . .	5	0	0
Sutton, Rev. F. . . .	5	0	0
Smyth, W. Esq. . . .	5	0	0
Stockdale, Capt. . . .	5	0	0
Strickland, Walter, Esq.	4	0	0
Sanders, Rev. T. . . .	1	0	0
Scott, G. G. Esq. . .	2	2	0
Sharpe, Mrs.	1	0	0
Skipwith, Rev. R. . .			
Smith, Mrs., Northampton	0	5	0
Stevens, Mr. W. . . .	2	2	0
Turnell, Mrs	15	0	0
Thornton, Rev. J. C.	10	0	0
Trotman, W. Esq. . .	5	0	0
Thompson, Mr. W. M. .	1	1	0
Tomalin, Mr. jun. . .	1	1	0
Tresslar, Mr. J. . . .	1	0	0

	£	s.	d.
Vyse, Rev. G. H. . . .	5	0	0
Vyse, Col. E. H. . . .	1	0	0
Whewell, Dr.	5	0	0
Watkins, Joreline, Esq.	150	0	0
Watkins, Rev. C. F. .	50	0	0
Watkins, Justinian, Esq.	10	0	0
Watkins, Miss E. . .	10	0	0
Watkins, Rear-Admiral .			
Watkins, Miss . . .	2	0	0
Windows. The Family for	53	0	0
Wood, T. Esq. . . .	210	0	0
Wood, Mr. Charles . .	5	0	0
Walter, Mr. C. . . .	2	0	0
Wales, Rev. Chancellor .	5	0	0
Watson. Mr., Harborough	2	0	0
Woolcomb, Rev. W. .	3	0	0
Wilson, Miss	1	0	0
Wallis, Owen, Esq. . .	5	0	0
Watson, Hon. Mrs. . .	1	0	0
Wickes, Rev. J. . . .	1	1	0
Wright, J. W. Esq. . .	2	2	0
Watts, Mr., Naseby .	1	0	0
Miss Watkins, Mrs. Gage,			
Mrs. Flood, Miss Bates,			
Mrs. Harper, &c., by			
cards	35	18	10
Loan from Public Works			
Loan Office	191	0	0
Total £2,476		0	0
Expended . . . £2,434		0	0
Memorial Windows .	53	0	0
£2,487		0	0

Expected further to receive about 70l.

THE END.

GILBERT AND RIVINGTON, PRINTERS, ST. JOHN'S SQUARE, LONDON.